## GREAT NECK LIBRARY
### GREAT NECK, N. Y.

# THE YEAR
# THEY WALKED

# THE YEAR THEY WALKED

## Rosa Parks and the Montgomery Bus Boycott

## BEATRICE SIEGEL

FOUR WINDS PRESS ❈ NEW YORK
MAXWELL MACMILLAN CANADA TORONTO
MAXWELL MACMILLAN INTERNATIONAL
NEW YORK OXFORD SINGAPORE SYDNEY

Four Winds Press
Macmillan Publishing Company
866 Third Avenue
New York, NY 10022

Maxwell Macmillan Canada, Inc.
1200 Eglinton Avenue East
Suite 200
Don Mills, Ontario M3C 3N1

Macmillan Publishing Company is part of the Maxwell Communication Group of Companies.

First edition. Printed and bound in the United States of America

10 9 8 7 6 5 4 3 2 1

The text of this book is set in 11 point Joanna. Book design by Christy Hale

---

Library of Congress Cataloging-in-Publication Data
Siegel, Beatrice. The Day They Walked: Rosa Parks and the Montgomery Bus Boycott /Beatrice Siegel. — 1st ed.
    p.    cm. Includes bibliographical references and index.
Summary: Examines the life of Rosa Parks, focusing on her role in the Montgomery bus boycott.
ISBN 0-02-782631-7
1. Parks, Rosa, 1913–  —Juvenile literature.  2. Afro-Americans—Alabama—Montgomery—Biography—Juvenile literature.  3. Civil rights workers—Alabama—Montgomery—Biography—Juvenile literature. 4. Montgomery (Ala.)—Biography—Juvenile literature.  5. Montgomery (Ala.)—Race relations—Juvenile literature.  6. Afro-Americans—Civil rights—Alabama—Montgomery—Juvenile literature. 7. Segregation in transportation—Alabama—Montgomery—History—20th century—Juvenile literature. [1. Parks, Rosa, 1913–  .  2. Afro-Americans—Biography.  3. Afro-Americans—Civil rights.] I. Title.
F334.M753P387  1992 323′.092—dc20 [B] 91-14078

For Constance Berkley,
my good friend
and patient teacher

# CONTENTS

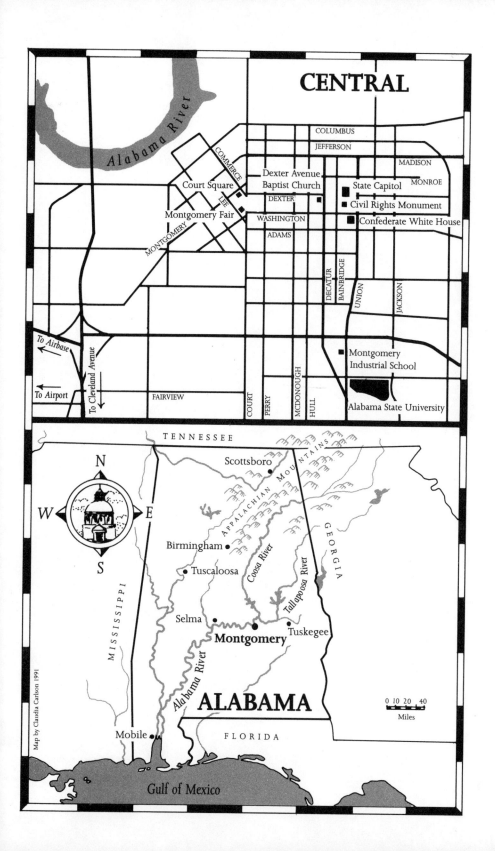

# 1

## AN ARREST

For the third day in a row cold winds roared through the South, driving the temperature down to below freezing. In Montgomery, Alabama, the extraordinary weather made front-page newspaper headlines. Except for that, the city went about its business of preparing for the Christmas season. Twinkling red and green lights and cheerful signs announcing preholiday sales made the city look festive. In the center of Court Square, a busy intersection in the heart of the business district, stood the magnificent old bronze fountain, graceful figures of goddesses perched around its edges. On a corner opposite the fountain, people were lined up for the buses to take them home at the end of the day.

It was not unusual for those waiting for a bus to hurry to the stores across the street to do some last-minute shopping. That was what Mrs. Rosa Parks did. She was a slim, attractive, forty-two-year-old woman dressed in a winter hat and coat and wearing rimless eyeglasses. December 1, 1955, had been an ordinary enough day for Mrs. Parks, though she was a bit tired that evening and bothered by a touch of bursitis in her shoulder. She had finished her day's work as a tailor's assistant at the Montgomery Fair, the town's leading department store. The hot, stuffy room in which she worked had been busy with the holiday rush. Before she lined up for the Cleveland Avenue bus, she did some shopping at Lee's Cut Rate Drug Store for items she needed at home.

When the Cleveland Avenue bus arrived, Mrs. Parks entered the front of the bus, dropped her ten-cent coin into a box, and found a seat. Often Mrs. Parks had to pay her coin, return to the street, and reboard the bus through the rear door. Mrs. Parks had to do that because she was black. In Montgomery, Alabama, only white people could always enter a bus through the front door.

That evening Mrs. Parks was lucky, for she found a seat in the crowded bus, an aisle seat in the first row of the colored section. The first ten seats in the front of the bus were reserved for whites, while blacks filled the back. If seats were vacant in the white section, blacks could not occupy them. Sometimes hard-working black people, their arms full of packages, would have to stand over an empty place in the white section. When whites were standing, however, blacks had to give up their seats. That was the law in Montgomery, and bus drivers, all of them white, had the power to enforce the rules.

Mrs. Parks was comfortable, her packages in her lap, as the bus rumbled on toward Cleveland Court, the housing complex where she lived. In fifteen minutes she would be home with her husband, Raymond, a barber, and her mother, who lived with them. Next to her sat a black man, and black women occupied the two seats across the aisle. Two stops later, near the Empire Theater, the bus was filled and a white man was standing. The back of the bus was packed with black people, many standing in the aisle.

The bus driver, James Blake, looked at the four black people sitting in the first row after the white section and called out that he wanted those seats. All four would have to give up their seats, for it was against the law for a black person to sit in the same row as a white.

No one moved. Blake called out again, "You all better make it light on yourselves and let me have those seats."

At that rebuke, the three people seated with Mrs. Parks moved to the rear of the bus. Mrs. Parks remained seated.

The bus driver came up to her and said, "Look, woman, I told you I wanted the seat. Are you going to stand up?"

"No, I'm not," said Mrs. Parks.

"Well, if you don't stand up, I'm going to have to call the police and have you arrested," said Blake.

Mrs. Parks would not move. "Go ahead and call them," she told the bus driver.

Blake got off the bus to call the police. A few minutes later two police officers were standing in front of Mrs. Parks. After confirming that she had understood the driver's request, one of the officers asked, "Why didn't you get up?"

"I didn't think I should have to," answered Mrs. Parks. And she added, "Why do you push us around?"

"I don't know, but the law is the law and you are under arrest," replied the officer.

The police put Mrs. Parks into a patrol car and drove her to city hall, where she was charged with breaking the law. From there she was taken to the city jail to be fingerprinted and photographed.

Witnessing the arrest was Mrs. Pratt, a neighbor of Mrs. Parks. Shocked by what had happened, she rushed home and phoned

Mrs. Bertha Butler. Mrs. Butler knew Mrs. Parks well, and she immediately phoned Mr. E. D. Nixon, a longtime civil rights leader and head of the local branch of the National Association for the Advancement of Colored People (NAACP).

While phones were ringing throughout the neighborhood, Mrs. Parks was in the city jail. She thought no one knew where she was. After a while she was permitted to phone home. Her mother asked immediately, "Did they beat you?"

Rosa Parks was in danger, and the black community knew it.

# 2

# SOUTHERN BEGINNINGS

S he did not see herself as heroic, Mrs. Parks would say, but simply as a woman who spoke up against segregation. Where did she find the courage to do it? What was her life like before that day in December 1955?

She was born to James and Leona McCauley in Tuskegee, Alabama, on February 4, 1913. They named her Rosa Louise. Her father was a carpenter and her mother a teacher. When Rosa was two, her father moved away. She, her mother, and her younger brother, Sylvester, moved in with her maternal grandparents, who had a small farm on the outskirts of Montgomery in a town called Pine Level.

Her early school education did not amount to much. Like most southern rural schools for blacks, hers in Pine Level was overcrowded and poorly equipped. Instead of windows, the room was fitted with wooden shutters through which light filtered. When the shutters were closed on cold days, the room was dark. No amount of hard work on the part of one teacher for all grades could brighten the barren room that had no heat, no water, and no indoor toilets.

A new school in the neighborhood was for white children only, and Rosa saw them driven back and forth each day in a bus. She had to walk miles to her school. That bus made an everlasting impression. In later years Mrs. Parks would say, "The bus was among the first ways I realized there was a black world and a white world."

Nor did Rosa's school run the full eight or nine months of a school year. Hers was let out after six or seven months so that children could work on the farms. That was what Rosa did, working alongside her grandparents in the fields, planting and picking cotton, peanuts, and seasonal crops that she helped sell at the markets.

Her childhood was helped along by the church, which became the backbone of her life. With her family she regularly attended services at the African Methodist Episcopal Church. It was more than a place of worship, more than a place where Rosa learned music and sang her favorite spirituals, "Oh Freedom, Let It Ring" and "Before I'd Be a Slave I'd Be Buried in My Grave." It was where people exchanged news in the absence of a local black newspaper. It was where you could get a loan if you needed one; where you felt safe, less threatened by the surrounding white community. The church was also the center for organizations such as mutual aid societies and social and political clubs. The church and its connected organizations created a sense of community, kept people closely knit, and fostered a feeling of solidarity.

In those growing years, Rosa thought only about getting through the dreadful pattern of the days. She was six years old when she learned about the Ku Klux Klan, or KKK, the nightriders cloaked in white sheets and hoods who terrorized the black neighborhoods. She heard the grown-ups talk of homes and churches burned to the ground, of people dragged from their beds and savagely whipped or killed. The talk among neighbors was not about integration, or politics, or of dreams for the future. They talked about how to survive the persecution, how to stay away from white people who battered their lives. Though her grandfather kept an old gun for protection, it did not reassure Rosa. She remained gripped by fear, tossing in her bed through sleepless nights.

Both her grandparents had been born into slavery, and Rosa learned from them about the terrible conditions in which they had lived. Her grandmother would describe how little slave children were fed. The food was poured from one huge pot in the yard, the way chickens and pigs were fed. Rosa's grandfather, a son of the slaveowner, was treated cruelly after his father died. Crippled early in life, he was beaten by the overseer and often went without shoes and clothing.

Rosa was ten when her grandfather died and again the family moved. This time they settled in with an aunt in Montgomery. Mrs. McCauley, who could not get a job as a teacher, worked in a beauty parlor and took in sewing to add to her income.

Living through those nightmarish days, Rosa tried hard to improve herself. She credits her mother with giving her the strength to endure, building up her sense of self-worth, helping her understand that she was as good as anyone else.

Mrs. McCauley, patient and nurturing, knew the importance of education. She saved up money to pay the small admission fee to a special school so that Rosa could take advantage of a better educational opportunity at the Montgomery Industrial School.

Rosa was eleven when she entered the fifth grade there. She became one of a student body of 325 black girls. The school building itself was impressive, a large brick structure with two floors of schoolrooms and facilities for children from kindergarten to the ninth grade. The school had been founded in 1886 by two northern white women, Miss H. Margaret Beard and Miss Alice L. White. They had been helped and supported by the American Missionary Society of New York and by other northern whites who wanted to do good deeds for southern blacks. At its peak the school had ten white women teachers, who, for daring to work with black children, were isolated by Montgomery's white population.

At the school Rosa received a solid education that included classes in literature. But the curriculum emphasized practical work, teaching the children a vocation: how to be homemakers. Rosa took courses in cooking, sewing, basketry, and embroidery, and she attended lectures on cleanliness and discipline. An emphasis on "Christian values" meant chapel meetings every Friday morning, filled with sermons and singing.

Schoolmates remember Rosa as a quiet, genial sort of young girl. Everyone was fond of her and thought she was easy to get along with. Many of the youngsters who attended the school would become women active in the community, in church work, civil rights, and voter registration.

When the school closed down in 1927, Rosa was in the seventh grade. She continued her education at the Booker T. Washington Junior High School, from which she graduated at age fifteen. From there she went on to Alabama State High School, an all-black school on the campus of the Alabama State College, which was also all black. Before graduation she had to drop out of school to help the family, especially to nurse her ailing mother and grandmother. She was nineteen when she married Raymond Parks in December 1932.

By trade Mr. Parks was a barber. He was also a courageous civil rights activist deeply involved in the Scottsboro case. In the North the case had become a crusade for justice. Mass meetings, picket lines, and letter-writing campaigns called for freedom for the nine black men, aged thirteen to twenty, accused of raping two white women in a freight car traveling through Alabama. The trial was held in the town of Scottsboro, in the northeast corner of Alabama. Despite evidence proving the young men innocent, a few were found guilty and sentenced to death. Others were sentenced to seventy-five to ninety-nine years in prison.

In racist Alabama, it was dangerous for Raymond Parks to be involved in the Scottsboro case. The state legal system was determined to put the men to death. Rosa would later recall secret meetings in their apartment when her husband was trying to raise money for the cause. Equally dangerous were Mr. Parks's work for the local branch of the National Association for the Advancement of Colored People, of which he was a charter member, and his work in voter registration. People had been killed in the South for helping black citizens exercise their right to vote.

The government made special efforts to prevent blacks from casting a ballot. Registrants had to answer a series of twenty-one questions, questions so difficult that highly educated people had trouble with them. Once that hurdle was passed, registrants had to pay all the poll taxes back to their twenty-first birthday. For poor people the sum was often considerable.

Soon after she was married, Rosa returned to high school, receiving her diploma in 1933. The thirties were the years of the Great Depression, and she had a hard time finding work, going from one low-paying job to another. For a while she was a clerk in an insurance company; for a while she was a domestic worker. After work hours she did sewing at home for private customers. Several years were spent at the Crittenden Tailor Shop before she went on to the Montgomery Fair as a tailor's assistant.

Throughout these years of hard work she was involved in civil rights. In 1943 she joined the NAACP and became secretary of the Montgomery chapter, where she met Edgar Daniel Nixon, president of the state branch. Mrs. Parks knew Mr. Nixon as the most militant person in Montgomery. He spoke to her about registering to vote, and in 1945—after her third try and after paying the total poll tax of eighteen dollars—she cast her first ballot.

The cases fought by the NAACP got no publicity. They were as invisible to the public and to history as if they had never occurred. But those who, like Rosa and Raymond Parks and Mr. Nixon, were fighting against the oppression of African-Americans saw brutal crimes against their people. There were cases dealing with "flogging, peonage, murder, and rape," as Mrs. Parks described them in an interview in Ebony magazine.

From the very beginning of her social and political work, Mrs. Parks was drawn to young people. She wanted to make their lives easier, to help them along. To do so she organized a youth council within the NAACP. At first the council had only five members, who attended meetings as much to eat Mrs. Parks's cookies as to learn community values. "She was a doer, not a bragger," said E. D. Nixon.

But her work with youth expanded and became central to her activism. She tutored youngsters and saw to it that they had the proper books and clothes for school. She helped them move forward and get on with their lives.

By the 1950s Mrs. Rosa Parks was well known in the community for her dedication to children and her work in civil rights and in the church. She had become an attractive woman with a deep sense of quiet. Within that quietude was enormous strength.

A rural Alabama school for black children in 1965 (Bruce Davidson/Magnum Photos, Inc.)

The Ku Klux Klan burning a cross to intimidate a community (*Bruce Roberts*)

Segregation of public toilets (*Bruce Roberts*)

Rosa Parks in 1954 (Photo by Ida Berman, courtesy Highlander Research and Education Center)

A school desegregation workshop at the Highlander Folk School. Septima Clark is second from left; Rosa Parks is second from right. (*Courtesy Highlander Research and Education Center*)

# 3

# THE CRADLE OF THE
# CONFEDERACY

S he needed that strength to live in Alabama. The state was
called the "heart of Dixie" because it had played a key role
in southern history.

Montgomery, located in the east-central part of the state, became the capital of Alabama in 1846. It was a beautiful city,
leaning on a bend in the Alabama River. Rolling hills led from
the town to the surrounding rich farmland known as the Black
Belt, a region that stretched clear across the central part of Alabama into the neighboring states of Georgia on the east and
Mississippi on the west.

The rich black soil grew cotton. The crop was so successful in
the years before the Civil War that it became the basis of the
economy and was said to rule the South. It also ruled the lives
of over two million black people under the system of slavery
that made its production possible.

In those long-ago years, Montgomery was a booming cotton
port. Barges and steamers drew up to the town piers to be
loaded with bales of cotton and sent majestically sailing down

the swift-running Alabama River through wide channels into the port of Mobile, on the Gulf of Mexico. From there cotton was shipped to other U.S. ports and on to Europe for the rapidly developing textile trade.

In the fight against slavery during the Civil War, Montgomery became the first capital of the Confederacy, as the southern states that seceded from the Union were called. Jefferson Davis was inaugurated as its first president on the steps of the white-pillared state house, over which the Confederate flag was unfurled.

Though slavery was abolished during the Civil War, racism was not abolished. It remained deeply embedded in southern life. In many ways it was another form of slavery. Millions of African-Americans continued to be the victims of a web of laws, rules, and customs that trapped them mercilessly in racial inequality. No matter what amendments were added to the Constitution or what new laws were adopted, the system of racism in the South remained untouched. "It was a struggle—just to be human," Rosa Parks would say, "to be a citizen, to have the rights and privileges of any other person."

In the face of continuous hardship, the black community had to define itself and the importance of its own culture, its humanity, its kindness. It had its own history and its daily struggles, rich with the beat of many voices saying things their own way. It had courageous citizens like E. D. Nixon and Raymond and Rosa Parks; young, articulate leadership in social and civic clubs; and strong clergymen in the many black churches.

Rosa Parks would recall those days and years in segregated Alabama as a time of "meager education, meager opportunities, economic deprivation, [and] rigid racial segregation" of all walks of life. In a newspaper interview in the *Chicago Tribune*, she would say that life was "just a matter of survival . . . of existing from one day to the next."

She hated it all the time, the inequality of her way of life—an inequality without reason. She dreamed "what it should be like to be a human being," she would tell an interviewer. So much was brutal and mean, she was often tired in body and soul. It would have been easier to fall apart than to care about what was going on. She would get "upset, angry many times, probably most of the time and many times discouraged," but she carried on. She would call it taking "one more step."

Along the hard road some events gave her courage and pushed her along. She saw black soldiers returning to the South after World War II and the Korean War put up a fight for the right to vote, seeking equal rights they felt they had won on the battlefields. Their struggle was crushed by white opposition, but it left its mark. People were aroused, increasingly angry and bitter.

In May 1954 came a stunning victory. In the case of Brown v. the Board of Education of Topeka, the U.S. Supreme Court ruled that school segregation was illegal. The victory brought wild rejoicing in the black communities. For many it was the first sign that the federal government was responding to their needs, that the promises of democracy might be realized. But 80 percent of the white people in the South opposed the ruling and vowed not to permit desegregation of schools. Alabama's governor sent in state troopers to enforce the segregation of schools, breaking the federal law.

Out of the backlash against the Brown decision, a new white hate group took root. Called the White Citizens Council, it was formed specifically to fight integration at every level and to terrorize black and white activists. The idea of mixing the races outraged these extremists. United States Senator James O. Eastland of Mississippi became a prominent figure in the organization, giving it national prominence. By the end of 1954 four Alabama counties had sprouted branches of the White Citizens

Council. In their newsletter they printed statements such as the following: "When in the course of human events it becomes necessary to abolish the Negro race, proper methods should be used. Among them are guns, bows and arrows, slingshots, and knives."

Desegregation of schools was now the law, but it would take a tremendous struggle to put the law into effect. Black people knew that there was no progress without struggle.

In July 1955, Mrs. Parks had a personal experience that helped her to overcome other barriers and added to her inner peace. On the recommendation of her friend Virginia Durr, a white woman whom Mrs. Parks knew well, she attended a school desegregation workshop at the Highlander Folk School in the hill country of Monteagle, Tennessee. The school was an independent adult-education center dealing with problems of social change. Founded by Myles Horton, it brought together black and white activists in trade unions and civil rights to discuss ways of reshaping southern life to achieve equality and justice for all races and classes.

Recalling her visit at a later date, Mrs. Parks would say that she had not been able to laugh for a long time. But Highlander changed all that. For the first time she experienced interracial living. It seemed natural for people, regardless of race, to live and work together. The thought came to her that there could be a unified society, "one of differing races and backgrounds meeting together . . . and living together in peace and harmony." She would say that at Highlander she gained the strength to persevere in her work for freedom, not just for blacks but for all oppressed people.

She also met Septima Clark at Highlander. Clark was a remarkable woman, clear in her vision and her struggles for equality. Parks was impressed with the ability of this black educator and teacher to organize and hold things together in an interracial setting. She admired Septima Clark for the very things she herself was not. "I was tense, and I was nervous, and I was upset most of the time.... I felt that I had been destroyed long ago. But I had the hope that young people could be benefited by equal education," she said in her remarks to the folksinger Pete Seeger for his book *Everybody Says Freedom*.

She was reluctant to leave Highlander. Where was she to go but back to segregated Montgomery and daily humiliation? Humiliation over something she could not control: the color of her skin.

A month after her return home, the brutal slaying of Emmett Till added to the terror in black communities. The fourteen-year-old youngster had come from Chicago to visit relatives in a small town in the neighboring state of Mississippi. On the evening of August 28, 1955, a gang of white men pulled the youngster from his bed, shot him through the head, and dumped his body into the Tallahatchie River. Why? Because, it was said, he dared address a white woman in the general store in a friendly way. The two men accused of and tried for the kidnapping and murder were found innocent.

By 1955 little had changed in Montgomery, Alabama, since the end of the 1880s, the period called Reconstruction that followed the Civil War. Other businesses had replaced the cotton trade, making Montgomery a center for small clothing factories, glass products, food products, and lumber mills. But in other ways, the town seemed to have been in a long sleep. It was still the Cradle of the Confederacy. Its favorite landmark was the white wooden house where Jefferson Davis lived while president.

The state of Alabama ranked as one of the worst—forty-seventh—in its system of education. It ranked high in poverty and infant deaths. Thousands of homes did not have running water. Schools for blacks remained ill-equipped one-room shacks. Schools for whites were better, though still below the national standards. Few funds were available for education, welfare, or any of the social services. Those who suffered most were the poor blacks and the poor whites. Nevertheless even the poor whites had a sense of power through the system of segregation, which told them they were better than the black people in town.

The division between black and white was still basic to the city's structure in 1955. Of Montgomery's population of some 140,000, about 50,000—36 percent—were black. They were confined to low-paying jobs. Men worked as ditch diggers, janitors, carpenters, gardeners, parking-lot attendants, or mechanics' assistants; or they worked in sawmills and lumber camps. The majority of black women who worked held jobs as cooks and maids in white homes, whereas the majority of white women who worked held jobs as clerical workers, a higher-paying category.

Though the majority of black people were poor, there was a small black middle and upper class. It was made up of businesspeople, store owners, insurance agents, and a handful of professionals: three physicians, one dentist, two lawyers, a pharmacist, and ninety-two clergymen. There were schoolteachers and college professors. In this class were many forceful people developing leadership skills. They were the ones who organized church and social clubs. They were the ones who formed committees to visit city officials to protest against injustice.

The upper class did not escape the laws of segregation. The color of a person's skin cut across all class lines, presenting the community with common problems and common handicaps.

Though they faced common problems, the black population was not united but separated by class differences. And in the small upper class there were also factions, organizations competing with each other for power in the community.

In his book *Stride Toward Freedom*, Martin Luther King, Jr., described how the city of Montgomery appeared to him when he settled there in 1954. He found a "threefold malady—factionalism among the leaders, indifference in the educated group, and passivity in the uneducated." The quiet acceptance of the way things were bothered him, though he understood that the passivity stemmed from fear: The black community was economically dependent on whites, and when an employee spoke up against segregation, that person often lost his or her job. He also understood the indifference as resulting from years of humiliation, a shattering of self-esteem brought about by a system that continuously told blacks they were inferior. On the surface the system of segregation was seldom challenged, making Montgomery appear as if it had solved the race question.

To an outside observer in the mid-1950s, the city would have looked calm and sunny, with breezes blowing off the river over the broad, tree-lined streets. The white-marble state capitol building gleamed on top of the hill, surrounded by administrative buildings. Montgomery was also the center of state and county governments, attracting lawyers and businesspeople attending to official business. Along the quiet upper-middle-class streets were spacious mansions and well-kept lawns and gardens. Two air-force bases on the outskirts of the city contributed to its economy.

White people were proud of Montgomery, proud of its historic tradition as the Cradle of the Confederacy. Steeped in custom and southern culture, they led genteel lives filled with old-fashioned courtesies. It pleased them that the Confederate flag still flew over the state capitol.

Underneath the surface of this glistening town, however, discontent simmered in the black community from years of repressed anger and bitterness. People vented their rage at the Montgomery City Lines bus company in particular, for that is where they experienced daily humiliation. Of the total black population of fifty thousand, about seventeen thousand rode the bus twice daily, to and from work. All the drivers were white, even though the majority of riders were blacks traveling through black neighborhoods. Among those drivers were nasty men who called black passengers offensive names. Riders were angry at the system of having to pay at the front of the bus and reboard at the rear, especially when some abusive drivers then rode off before passengers could reboard. They were also fed up with having to stand over empty seats in the white section.

Rosa Parks had had humiliating experiences on the buses before her arrest, and she did not like using them. Twelve years earlier, she had gotten on the bus, and after she paid her fare the driver, the same James Blake, insisted that she get off and re-board in the rear. When she refused to do so, Blake took her by the arm and escorted her off the vehicle. Rather than get back on that bus, she waited for another. She found bus transportation so degrading that she walked whenever possible.

The bus was only one part of the whole system, a system of segregation in every walk of life. It was the way white people held on to their power, and it was protected by law. To main-tain the system, there were police beatings, the terror of the White Citizens Councils, the KKK burnings of homes and churches, and lynchings. Between the years 1889 and 1941, close to four thousand lynchings took place in the South. Black parents taught their children not to challenge the laws of white society, for death lay in that direction.

The simple word "no" uttered by Mrs. Parks on December 1 threatened the whole rigid social structure of segregation. Mrs. Parks was saying that she was equal to the white man, that she had as much right to the bus seat as he did.

She had not known the exact moment or place she would choose to assert her sense of equality. Nor was it her intention at that moment to integrate the buses. All she wanted was to get home, be with her family, and carry on with the evening's plans.

She had fought a daily battle to maintain a sense of self, to value herself. The family, the church, the community, and her experiences at Highlander had helped her along the way. So had courageous leaders like E. D. Nixon and others fighting lonely battles.

# 4

# "STAY OFF THE BUSES
# ON MONDAY"

Phones rang, neighbors gathered, and the community came alive with the news: Rosa Parks was arrested.

"They arrested the wrong person," said E. D. Nixon. He knew Rosa Parks well. He knew the depth of her strength and her commitment to justice.

Nixon himself was fearless. A tall, impressive man, well over six feet, he was born and raised in Montgomery. In the poor family of seventeen children in which he grew up, his education ended at the seventh grade. Still, he became the civil rights leader of the black community. When others were afraid to speak up, he spoke for them, making use of special connections he had developed with people in power.

His job as a Pullman porter on overnight trains often took him out of town on runs to Chicago. The neighborhood knew him as a devoted member of the Brotherhood of Sleeping Car Porters, the trade union to which he belonged. Nixon would credit A. Philip Randolph, the national head of the Brotherhood, with giving him the strength to stand up as a trade unionist and as a leader in the fight against injustice. The community also knew Nixon as an NAACP leader and as president of the Progressive Democratic Association.

When he heard the news of Rosa Parks's arrest, he phoned the police station. He was unable to get a reply. In effect, he was told that it was none of his business. Fred Gray, one of the two black Montgomery lawyers, was out of town, so Nixon phoned a liberal white lawyer he knew well, Clifford Durr. Both Durr and his wife, Virginia, were outspoken in their opposition to segregation and were active in the Council on Human Relations, an interracial organization in Montgomery.

Durr reported back to Nixon that Rosa Parks had been arrested for refusing to give up her seat on the bus, a violation of a city ordinance giving drivers the right to decide seating on a city bus. Durr offered to go with Nixon to the police station, and Virginia Durr insisted on going along too. It was "a terrible sight," said Mrs. Durr, "to see this gentle, lovely, sweet woman, whom I knew and was so fond of, being brought down by a matron."

When Raymond Parks arrived to take his wife home, Nixon and the Durrs accompanied them. Over coffee at the Parks's apartment, they all discussed the arrest. Mrs. Parks had not only broken a segregation law but was almost guilty of another violation when she became thirsty in jail and wanted to drink out of the water fountain. It was for whites only, she was told.

That evening Nixon carefully suggested that the Parks arrest could be the case to challenge the seating arrangements in buses—with a boycott of the bus line! The idea was explosive. Who knew where a boycott would lead? Mrs. Parks's family, fearing for Rosa's safety, was upset. As the center of a case challenging state and city segregation laws, she could be lynched. But Mrs. Parks calmed her husband and her mother and agreed that her arrest could be used as a test case. Fred

Gray, who had returned to Montgomery that evening, would represent her in the appeal to the state courts. At Gray's side throughout the complicated process would be Clifford Durr and a group of experienced black lawyers from other cities.

That same Thursday evening, a different scene was being acted out in another part of town. Mrs. Jo Ann Robinson heard of the arrest through a late-night phone call from Fred Gray. A bright, energetic English professor at Alabama State College, she was an acknowledged leader in town. At the time of the Rosa Parks arrest, she was president of the Women's Political Council. The organization had been formed in 1946 by Alabama State professor Mary Fair Burks to work on voter registration and, in general, to try to maintain self-esteem in the black community in the face of daily insults.

Like many other women, Mrs. Robinson had had her own humiliating experiences on Montgomery City Line buses. In her memoirs she tells of an incident during one Christmas vacation when she boarded a bus to the local airport. Her arms were filled with packages, gifts she was taking to friends in Cleveland. Deep in thought, she forgot for a moment where she was and sat down in the front of the bus. In an instant, before she could collect her thoughts, she heard the booming voice of the bus driver shouting at her: "Get up from there! Get up from there!" Shaken by the angry voice and the menacing gestures of the driver, who looked as if he were ready to strike her, she fled from the bus, dropping her packages.

"I felt like a dog," she said. "And I got mad, after this was over, and I realized that I was a human being, and just as intelligent and far more trained than that bus driver. . . . I cried all the way to Cleveland."

At that time Mrs. Robinson vowed she would do everything possible to end the abuses on the buses. On several occasions the Women's Political Council had met with city officials to protest the behavior of the bus drivers and the needless indignity of having to pay at the front of the bus and reboard at the rear. The council also protested the regulation requiring blacks to stand over empty seats in the white section. Their protests were to no avail.

Several times in 1955 women had been forced to give up their seats on the buses. When they refused to do so they were arrested. Women usually paid the fine and did nothing more. But high-school student Claudette Colvin was different. She said she was tired of standing for white folks every morning. When she refused to give up her seat one day, police officers tried to arrest her. In resisting the arrest, she scratched the face of a policeman. She was handcuffed, taken off to jail, and kept there until the middle of the night. Not even her family knew where she was.

The incident caused an uproar in the community. The Women's Political Council was ready to make a test case of the arrest when it was discovered that Colvin was pregnant.

"Women were ready to explode" at the accumulation of insults, said Mrs. Robinson. More than once they had thought of boycotting the bus line. When Mrs. Robinson heard of the Parks arrest, she immediately got busy. She knew Mrs. Parks to be the right person: She was respected, hard-working, and she could stand up under pressure. Mrs. Robinson and Mr. Nixon readily agreed that Mrs. Parks could well be the one around whom they might bring about a change in the community. They decided to call a one-day boycott to take place on Monday, the day of the trial. But how to get the news around? Mrs. Robinson said she would get a flier out to the public. Mr. Nixon said he would arrange a meeting of black ministers and other leaders for the next day.

Mrs. Robinson called on her colleagues in the council, and a committee of women drew up a leaflet. It asked "every Negro to stay off the buses Monday in protest of the arrest and trial of Rosa Parks. Don't ride the buses to work, to town, to school, or anywhere on Monday," the leaflet urged.

Through a network of council members in all the schools, students helped distribute some 35,000 leaflets. They rang doorbells and visited homes, schools, shops, bars, and restaurants in the black community.

In the meantime, Nixon contacted black ministers with the assistance of Ralph D. Abernathy, the twenty-nine-year-old pastor of the First Baptist Church and secretary of the Baptist Ministers Alliance. Through the alliance, Abernathy could reach all the Baptist leaders in town. He himself was a forceful man and an effective public speaker. After serving in the U.S. Army in World War II, he became an educator and then studied for the ministry. Bright and vigorous, he used his talents in the crusade for progress for African-Americans.

Abernathy suggested the fashionable Dexter Avenue Baptist Church as a meeting place. It had a new pastor named Martin Luther King, Jr. At first the Reverend King hesitated about having the meeting there. He was new to the pastorate and felt pressured by many responsibilities. But he quickly realized the emergency nature of the boycott and agreed to let his church be used for the meeting.

Fifty community leaders were present Friday evening, December 2. Among them were ministers, heads of social and political clubs, businessmen, and teachers, making up a basic network for spreading the news. By the time of the meeting, leaflets calling for a boycott of buses on Monday, December 5, had already blanketed numerous neighborhoods. Faced with an accomplished fact, the group moved forward with plans to put out another 7,000 leaflets to be sure that every part of the city was covered. They also laid plans for alternate methods of transportation, setting up car pools and arranging for pickup stations. They called on the eighteen Negro taxicab companies, with two hundred cabs available. Plans were also made to hold a mass meeting Monday night after the day's boycott to decide on a future course of action. The mass meeting would be held in the community's largest hall, the Holt Street Baptist Church, which could hold hundreds of people.

Mrs. Parks attended the Friday-evening meeting. Though her friend E. D. Nixon was out of town on a trip to Chicago, she was warmly received and made comfortable. She spoke before the group, telling of her bus experience. That morning, the day after the arrest, she had shown up for work at the Montgomery Fair to the surprise of the other employees. They had seen the news item tucked away on page nine of the *Montgomery Advertiser*, the city's leading newspaper:

Negro Jailed Here
for 'Overlooking'
Bus Segregation

The article went on to tell about the arrest and pointed directly to "the woman, Rosa Parks, [of] 634 Cleveland Ave. . . ." A letter appeared in the *Advertiser* in response to the story. "Bring back the Klan," that was what Alabama needed, it said.

Tensions were rising in the black community. People were edgy working out alternate ways of getting to work. Rallying behind them were the wealthy people who owned their own cars. Those cars, needed for transportation, would become an important factor in the day's outcome.

On Sunday, December 4, news of the boycott was announced from every pulpit in every black church. The ministers explained that this radical step was a way of protesting the system of transportation that brutalized and humiliated Montgomery's black citizens every day. More than any other institution, the bus system was a reminder of their "inferiority," an attack on their dignity. The boycott was called, explained the ministers, not only to protest the arrest of Mrs. Rosa Parks but to make a statement for freedom. They were demanding their basic human rights.

Those who did not attend church would learn about the boycott in an unexpected way: through the pages of the *Montgomery Advertiser*. E. D. Nixon had leaked the story to Joe Azbell, the city editor. Azbell ran a front-page news item:

Negro Groups
Ready Boycott
of City Lines

The article referred to the leaflets flooding the streets and also announced the meeting set for Monday night at the Holt Street Baptist Church.

From pulpits, street corners, newspapers, telephones, and word of mouth, the call went out to the entire black community of 50,000: STAY OFF THE BUSES ON MONDAY IN PROTEST OF THE ARREST AND TRIAL OF ROSA PARKS.

# 5

## "NOW IS THE TIME"

Acold, bitter wind blew through the city on Monday, December 5. Rosa Parks, Martin Luther King, Jr., Jo Ann Robinson, and E. D. Nixon peered through their windows or stood on street corners, watching the big yellow buses roll down the streets. They were empty—empty of black riders, except for a few here and there. It was a miracle, said Dr. King. "The once dormant and quiescent Negro community was now fully awake." It was "the beginning of a new age for an oppressed people," said another black minister.

The city, to keep the buses full, had arranged for two motorcycle policemen to follow each bus to be sure that black "goons" were not intimidating riders. Other policemen guarded bus stops. But these ruses did not work. The boycott was a success.

At Court Square, where Rosa Parks had boarded the bus on the fateful evening of December 1, a handwritten sign was tacked onto the wall of the bus shed: PEOPLE, DON'T RIDE THE BUS TODAY. DON'T RIDE IT FOR FREEDOM.

In the downtown area of the city, black people were waiting on street corners for rides. Bundled up in winter coats and sweaters against the cold, wet day, many jammed into cars with volunteer drivers who stopped to pick them up. Or they piled into black-owned taxis at an agreed-upon fare of ten cents, the same fare paid on buses. They climbed onto pickup trucks. Thousands walked, lunch bags in their hands. Schoolchildren accompanied by parents walked the mile or more to school. High-school and college students walked or thumbed a ride. A few horsedrawn carriages and muledrawn carts appeared on the streets. The long walk had begun in Montgomery.

At eight o'clock that same morning, fifty black people gathered near the Recorder's Court, where the Rosa Parks trial was to take place. By the time court opened, the crowd had swelled to over five hundred, overflowing from the courtroom into hallways and streets. Accompanied by E. D. Nixon and her lawyer, Fred Gray, Mrs. Parks entered the court. Within five minutes the proceedings took place and ended. Tried on an old city code provision regulating bus segregation, she was found guilty, fined ten dollars and court costs of four dollars, and freed on a $100 bond. Her lawyer announced that he would appeal the case.

On Monday afternoon, the leaders of the boycott met to prepare the agenda for the mass meeting to be held that evening at the Holt Street Baptist Church. Exuberant over the success of the boycott, they saw the need for a new organization, one that would unite the black community and confront city officials with their demands. They called the new organization the Montgomery Improvement Association (MIA) and elected Martin Luther King, Jr., as the first president. An executive committee would carry on the work.

The Reverend King was not only new to the community and an inexperienced minister; he had been married only two years before, to the talented and beautiful Coretta Scott, and he was a new father. Baby Yolanda Denise had been born on November 17.

The twenty-six-year-old pastor had come from a background of strong family figures and religious leaders. His grandfather had been a Baptist minister, as was his father. Young Martin—or Mike, as he was called—grew up in an upper-middle-class family in Atlanta, Georgia, and had the advantages of a superior education. After graduating from Morehouse College, he went on to Crozer Theological Seminary, where he was class valedictorian and was awarded his bachelor of divinity degree in 1951. Given a scholarship for further education, he entered the Boston University School of Theology for a doctorate in philosophy.

In physical appearance, the young minister was a short, solemn-faced man. His many years of education and philosophical discussions gave him a thoughtful air during his first year in Montgomery, as if he had to ponder every aspect of a question. At all times his manner was unassuming, for he himself did not appreciate his power.

He was appointed to his first position in September 1954, when he became pastor of the Dexter Avenue Baptist Church in Montgomery. It was an old church built eighty years before during the Reconstruction period. The simple red-brick building stood on the corner of Montgomery's busiest thoroughfare. Dexter Avenue stretched from Court Square, with the fountain in its center, up the hill to the state capitol building on top of the slope. One block below the capitol, the Dexter Avenue Church stood in full view of the Confederate flag flying over the white-marble State House. The church was an enclave for the black elite, for college professors, businesspeople, professionals, and others prominent in the black community.

During his first year as minister, Dr. King had won over his parishioners. He was patient, persuasive, and responsible in caring for the needs of his congregation. He was an extraordinary orator, his words sparkling with knowledge that came from hundreds of books and philosophical discussions. His sermons, too, rolled with the voices of biblical figures and with the ancient history of his people. His deep passion for social issues had not yet been tapped, but he knew some things for certain. He wanted freedom and justice for all African-Americans. He also knew that violence was not an answer to their problems, not an answer to the violence visited on them by whites through history. Violence was not the way of God.

His first leadership role, as president of the Montgomery Improvement Association, would change the Reverend Martin Luther King, Jr. The movement would force him to grow in unexpected ways. And though at first people were not sure of him—who was he?—he had behind him the aura of the prestigious Dexter Avenue Church. And because he was a newcomer to the community, his slate was clean. He had not taken sides in local controversies.

The ministers at the Monday-afternoon meeting were uncertain about whether to continue the boycott. They would let those attending the mass meeting that night decide. In the upheaval over the Rosa Parks arrest, the community was experiencing growing pains, working together for the first time. If nothing else happened, the successful boycott that day would write a glorious chapter to history.

The day had been so busy that Dr. King did not have time to prepare his talk for the evening. He was deep in thought as he approached the Holt Street Baptist Church and at first could not understand why traffic and dense crowds of people were blocking the streets. Rosa Parks, too, had difficulty getting into the church, and Virginia and Clifford Durr could not get through the crowds at all. They had to turn back.

Over five thousand people had spilled from the church and overflowed into the streets. They stood jammed together, a diverse crowd, people of different religious beliefs, social values, and classes: the laborer and the professional, the domestic worker and the upper-class lady. Through them ran a current of energy, strength, and good cheer. They felt a kinship to each other through their concern for Rosa Parks and their elation over the success of the day's boycott.

The mass meeting started with the audience standing to sing the hymn "Onward, Christian Soldiers." They sang in rapturous choral voices, the massive sounds coming from both within and outside the church. After prayers, E. D. Nixon said a few words from the podium, urging everyone to be strong, to "stand on our feet and take our rightful place in society."

The Reverend Martin Luther King, Jr., was called on to give the main talk. He stood at the pulpit of the church, facing the intent audience, aware of the thousands who would hear him over the loudspeakers. "We are here because we are American citizens," he said in his opening sentences, "and we are determined to apply our citizenship to the fullness of its means." He went on to talk about the practical situation before them: the arrest of Rosa Parks. "I'm happy that it happened to a person like Mrs. Parks," he said, "for nobody can doubt the boundless outreach of her integrity. Nobody can doubt the height of her character. Nobody can doubt the depth of her Christian commitment. . . ."

The words began to flow. They pulsed with the man's eloquence. "There comes a time," he said, "when people get tired of being trampled over by the iron feet of oppression." Excitement surged through the crowd, enthusiasm breaking out in a chorus of "Yes! Yes!" and "Amen!" As Dr. King continued to speak, he looped his words together into a new beat. The thousands listening to him cheered him on with their shouts of

"Amen!" And while the cheering and shouting were going on, King's voice continued to ring out. "There comes a time, my friends, when people get tired of being flung across the abyss of humiliation where they experience the bleakness of nagging despair," he said. "There comes a time when people get tired of being pushed out of the glittering sunlight of life's July and left standing amidst the piercing chill of an alpine November." He called for dignity, for staying united as they stood up for their rights. "We must stick together and work together," he cautioned, "if we are to win . . . our rights as Americans."

Speaking from the depths of his own soul, he touched his listeners' terrible pain and heartache. He spoke against the use of violence, maintaining that the only weapon they had was the "weapon of protest." He quoted from the Bible, saying that they were determined in Montgomery to work and fight "until justice rolls down like waters and righteousness like a mighty stream."

At that first mass meeting, King introduced a new approach to the civil rights struggle. In his vision, love was the guiding star. Blacks must not hate their white opponents while they sought justice. Instead, he urged his listeners to have compassion and good will toward whites. This approach was known as nonviolent resistance, and it would develop into a social force and a powerful weapon of protest.

King also emphasized the need for unity, the need to work together. "Right here in Montgomery when the history books are written in the future, somebody will have to say, 'There lived a race of people, of black people, . . . of people who had the moral courage to stand up for their rights.' "

After the young pastor's forceful talk, the evening reached another emotional peak with the introduction of Rosa Parks, to thunderous applause and a standing ovation. People saw in Mrs. Parks a symbol of their hopes and aspirations. This shy-looking woman had put up a fight—could they do less?

In describing the Holt Street mass meeting, city editor Joe Azbell reported in the *Montgomery Advertiser* that he had never heard such singing. "They were on fire for freedom. There was a spirit there that no one could capture again . . . it was so powerful."

Jo Ann Robinson (*Courtesy Booker T. Lee*)

The Reverend Martin Luther King, Jr., addressing a meeting of the MIA. The Reverend Ralph Abernathy is in the first row on the left; Rosa Parks is seated next to him. (Don Cravens)

Motorcycle police watch a black-owned parking lot where people gathered
for rides (*Don Cravens*)

Fred Gray (left), the Reverend Ralph Abernathy (center), and the Reverend
Robert Graetz (right) discuss boycott business (AP/Wide World Photos)

Rosa Parks fingerprinted by a deputy sheriff in February 1956, at time of arrest of over one hundred in boycott case (*AP/Wide World Photos*)

E. D. Nixon and Rosa Parks entering the courthouse in bus boycott case
(*AP/Wide World Photos*)

The Reverend Martin Luther King, Jr., addressing a mass meeting (*Collection of Bayard Rustin*)

# 6

# THE YEAR THEY WALKED

The thousands gathered in the Holt Street Baptist Church and on the streets gave the leadership its answer: Continue the boycott!

Resolutions passed at the meeting called on all citizens to stay off the buses owned by the City Lines bus company until demands were met. Those demands were announced by the Reverend Ralph Abernathy. They had been drawn up in the afternoon by members of the Montgomery Improvement Association and asked for the following changes:

1. Blacks were to sit in buses from the back forward, whites from the front backward. No one would have to give up a seat, and no one would have to stand while seats were empty.
2. Bus drivers were to be courteous to all riders.
3. Blacks, who represented 75 percent of all riders, should be able to apply for jobs as drivers.

The demands were so modest that they did not even include a call to end segregated seating on the buses. Further resolutions enlisted car owners to help people get to work; asked employers to help transport their employees; and called for a delegation to try to meet with the bus company to discuss the demands.

The movement was in the hands of the MIA and its executive board of forty-six people, over half of whom were ministers. They had always provided a network that knit the community together. But now, instead of ministering to a troubled congregation, they were dealing with a rebellious people.

On the board were several women, among them Mrs. Jo Ann Robinson, who would be the publicist for the movement. There was also Mrs. A. W. West, a dynamic leader and wife of the only black dentist in town. Others on the board included physicians, college professors, labor leaders, and one white, the Reverend Robert Graetz.

But the success or failure of the movement rested on some seventeen thousand black people who rode the buses twice a day. They were ordinary people, people who would never become famous, people who could not afford to miss a day's work. They were the ones who would face employers who insulted them and motorcycle cops who threatened and harassed them as they filed into cars and taxis. They were the disciplined ones who would attend mass meetings twice a week, patiently listening to talks advising them not to be violent, to turn the other cheek. They would convert the boycott into a mass movement, filling it out with their anger and bitterness over years of racial incidents. As they took charge of their own lives, their strength would sweep like a tide over everyone. They had waited a long time for change.

The struggle exploding around Mrs. Parks had become larger

than the single person, though the movement would not forget that she had led the way and cast a spotlight on the city of Montgomery.

Within a few days of the Holt Street mass meeting, Montgomery became known as the "walking city." Thousands were seen hurrying along to their jobs on foot. Some walked as far as twelve miles a day to their places of work and back home.

To make the boycott a success took more than determination and help from a few white employers. It took practical planning, which evolved with time. It took the daily, plodding work of a small staff paid by church collections and groups of volunteers. Together, they put into operation a smooth-running system of alternate methods of transportation.

The most important job was that of chair of the transportation committee. For the first few months Rufus Lewis, a wealthy businessman, took on the work. Dedicated to the community, active in voter registration, he owned his own business and could not be affected by the white power structure. He was replaced after several months by the Reverend B. J. Simms, an ordained Baptist minister and professor of history and philosophy at Alabama State College.

A downtown parking lot owned by a black man became the central command post for a fleet of cars that operated like shared taxicabs. Within weeks some three hundred vehicles were in the car pool. Financial recordkeeping was tightened so that the few who tried to abuse the system by collecting fares twice or getting more gas than needed were disciplined. In the tight organization, certified shops were designated to handle all repairs, and careful records were kept.

Black churches became shelters for thirty-two morning dispatch stations and forty-one afternoon and evening pickup stations. People could wait indoors in bad weather. Street corners were also designated as pickups as the system expanded. Three dispatchers were put on the staff. Their goal was for all black workers and their families to be able to get from one place to another without using a city bus.

Committees of volunteers sprang into action: volunteers who used their cars for transportation; volunteers who cooked for the boycotters; women who staffed the office, or acted as dispatchers, secretaries, and clerks. Among the active women were Mrs. Ann Pratt, chief assistant to Professor Simms. Mrs. A. W. West drove her green Cadillac through the neighborhoods in the car pool. Mrs. Johnnie Carr, an energetic woman, also drove her car through the streets, giving people lifts. Black soldiers and three white ones from the nearby Maxwell Air Force Base helped out in the car pool.

The huge, orderly plan surprised the white community. Here was a new movement, led and staffed by black people, providing an effective alternate system of transportation for thousands. White support was minimal, coming from those who privately contributed money. In the first months the financial needs were met by the small contributions from the mass of blacks. Months later funds would come from all over the state and, finally, from the entire country.

Through the changing seasons, through the winter, spring, summer, and fall of 1956, the black population of Montgomery thumbed a ride, or used a car pool or station wagon, or walked to and from their jobs. Through it all, people acted and moved together, filled with high spirits and self-respect as they saw their actions turning the city around. The empty buses rolling by told them the boycott was a success.

"My feet are tired," said one woman, "but my soul is rested." Another woman, rejecting the offer of a ride, explained, "I'm walking for my children and my grandchildren."

# 7

# BACKLASH

Not until the fourth day of the boycott, Thursday, December 8, did a meeting take place between the delegates of the MIA and city officials. Representing the MIA at the meeting were the Reverends King and Abernathy, lawyer Fred Gray, Mrs. Robinson, and eight others. Present for the city were Mayor W. A. Gayle and two city commissioners. Acting for the bus company were James H. Bagley and Jack Crenshaw, the company lawyer.

Dr. King, speaking for the MIA, explained that the demands were moderate, since they were asking only for a more just system and not for the end of segregation. He placed before them demands similar to those approved at the Holt Street meeting: that blacks were to take seats in the bus from the back to the front, while whites occupied seats from the front to the back; the last to come would occupy whatever seats were available between the two. He also asked for better treatment by bus drivers and the hiring of black drivers on buses covering black neighborhoods.

After days of negotiation, the MIA won a minor concession. Crenshaw agreed that abusive bus drivers would be reprimanded. He would introduce no further changes, however. The time was not ripe, he said. City officials were afraid that if they made any concessions, no matter how small, black people would want everything changed. "Give them an inch and they'll take a mile" was the general attitude.

The MIA leaders began to see that they would have to forge ahead to a new level and challenge the segregation laws themselves in order to win new seating arrangements on city buses. In the first weeks of the boycott they were not ready for such a step. The whole situation was new—would it hold together?

Empty buses were rolling along the streets. Seventy-five percent of their former riders were black and were involved in the boycott. The company reported a loss of sixty-five percent of its income, which came to thousands of dollars. Still the whites were uncompromising, though increasingly frustrated by the strength of the boycott. To crush it became their goal.

They started off by spreading rumors. They said the boycott leadership was getting rich, making money from the protest movement. Then they said there was infighting among the leaders, with young ones pushing the older ones out.

When rumors did not work, police began to arrest black drivers of taxis and autos and charge them with speeding. They targeted drivers going thirty miles per hour in a twenty-five-mile zone. They also stopped overloaded cars. Jo Ann Robinson was given seventeen tickets in a few months.

They also began to harass black cab drivers who were charging passengers ten cents a ride, demanding that taxis charge the minimum rate of forty-five cents a fare. Boycotters could not pay that. To get around the new ruling, the MIA made a special plea to owners of private automobiles, asking them to chauffeur people to their jobs. There were hundreds of volunteers. Some white women drove their maids to and from their jobs rather than do the heavy household work themselves.

As the boycott went on, the business district and the economy of white Montgomery began to feel the economic pinch. Black people not only stopped taking buses, they stopped shopping in downtown stores. Despite the serious downward slide in the city's finances, white officials would make no concessions. The Reverend King, however, made a concession on behalf of the MIA. He proposed to postpone the demand for the employment of black drivers until a later date.

The Monday- and Thursday-night meetings became the rallying ground for boycotters and their leadership. They increasingly took on the form of a combination protest rally and church service. Crowds arrived early in order to get a seat. They sang, prayed, talked to each other, or read a book or newspaper until the meeting started. After hymn singing and scripture reading, Dr. King would give an update on the boycott's progress. He would be followed by the Reverend Abernathy, who discussed future strategies. People spoke up, giving their opinions. The meeting ended with a pep talk, exhorting everyone to remain disciplined and united. Boycotters were asked not to be violent, and to resist all provocations by whites.

While blacks were developing a nonviolent philosophy, whites were moving in the opposite direction. The boycott was in its fourth week on January 6 when the White Citizens Council held a meeting in Montgomery. Twelve hundred people jammed the hall. At the meeting, Police Commissioner Clyde Sellers announced to a standing ovation that he was joining the council. Two weeks later, on January 24, Mayor Gayle and City Commissioner Frank Parks also announced that they had joined the White Citizens Council. In making public their membership in a coercive, segregationist organization, city officials were warning the black community that they would stop at nothing to break the boycott.

Though many in the protest movement were frightened by this turn of events, unity remained strong even when the council began to exert economic pressure. Blacks could no longer get bank loans, and many lost their jobs, among them Rosa Parks, who was fired from the Montgomery Fair.

Hardships increased, for many black people were dependent on whites for their livelihood. Those few whites who were friendly to boycotters were isolated and harassed. The Reverend Graetz, the young white pastor of the Negro Trinity Lutheran Church, had his car vandalized. Prowlers broke windows in his home. Violence escalated, with threatening phone calls to the leaders. The Reverend King was a favorite target, as was Rosa Parks.

In the face of the stepped-up harassment, the MIA announced additional mass meetings. At the same time, Police Commissioner Sellers, addressing a meeting of businessmen, vowed that it was important to maintain their way of life. "What they [black people] are after is the destruction of our social fabric," he announced to the white population, and he vowed to pursue every means to stop them.

Police dispersed groups of blacks waiting for car rides on street corners. Mayor Gayle singled out for criticism the white women who continued to give rides to black domestic workers despite his plea that they stop doing so. He wanted to be sure that absolutely nothing was done to aid the "Negro radicals," as he called the leadership directing the boycott.

Police began to trail taxis and cars filled with black people, giving them traffic tickets for nonexistent or trivial violations. One victim was the Reverend King, stopped by a police car and given a summons for speeding though he was going only thirty miles per hour. He was put into a patrol car and driven through lonely streets to a distant jail. Placed in a filthy cell, he was treated like a common criminal, taken out and fingerprinted. Word spread quickly, and a group of colleagues hurried to the jail to bail him out.

When these forms of harassment failed to halt the boycott, violence exploded with the bombing of the Kings' house on the evening of January 30. Dr. King was away at the time, speaking at a church meeting. But Coretta Scott King and a friend, Mrs. Mary Lucy Williams, were home, and two-month-old baby Yolanda was asleep in a back room. The two women heard a loud thud, as if something heavy had landed on the porch, and they heard footsteps. Alarmed, they both rushed to the back of the house. They had barely retreated to the other room when an explosion shattered the glass in the living room, sending fragments shooting in all directions and filling the house with smoke. After making sure the baby was safe, Mrs. King phoned the church to alert Dr. King of the bombing. A neighbor phoned the police.

When he got the news, Dr. King rushed home to find hundreds of neighbors and supporters gathered in front of the house, wanting to make sure the family was not hurt. The mayor, police commissioner, and fire chief were all there, examining the damage of the blast, but they could not restrain the anger of the crowd, enraged at the violence against the King family.

Only Dr. King could calm them. Standing on the porch of the parsonage, the mayor and police chief on either side of him, he assured his supporters that his family was unharmed. He urged that they do nothing violent to the white community. "If you have weapons, take them home. . . . We must meet violence with nonviolence," he said. He ended his talk saying, "I want it to be known the length and breadth of this land that if I am stopped this movement will not stop. If I am stopped our work will not stop. For what we are doing is right. What we are doing is just. And God is with us."

"God bless you, Brother King," the crowd shouted.

# 8

# FRIENDS AND ALLIES

After eight weeks of increasing violence, the MIA and its lawyers, Fred Gray and Charles Langford, decided to attack the matter from a different angle. On February 1, they filed suit in U.S. district court seeking an injunction, or order, against segregated bus seating. In their suit, they asked specifically that the Montgomery city code of 1952 requiring racial segregation on transportation facilities be declared unconstitutional.

On the same day the brief was filed, the home of E. D. Nixon was bombed, in spite of promises by the mayor to find and punish those who had bombed the King home just two days before. Nixon was away, but his wife, Arlet, and a neighbor's seven-year-old child were in the house. They escaped injury.

In the increasing violence, Dr. King and Mrs. Parks were singled out for a flood of hate mail and nasty phone calls. Each day the King family received thirty to forty calls from unidentified persons who cursed and insulted them. Postcards filled with brief messages and signed "KKK" threatened their lives. "Get out of town, or else" was the gist of the messages. The family, shaken by the hate mail and threats, could get neither sleep nor rest. But they did not give in, despite the urgent pleading of both Dr. King's and Mrs. King's parents. Both fathers had rushed to Montgomery when they heard of the bombing and insisted that the young family return to Atlanta, where they would be safe. Dr. King explained that he could not do that; his place was among his people.

As the threats grew more frequent, Dr. King experienced a terrible fear that either he or some family member would be killed. One night he was not sure he had the strength to go on. During hours of personal anguish and prayer, he overcame his fears and knew that thereafter, no matter what happened, his life belonged to the struggle for justice.

For Mrs. Parks and her family it was a costly victory. When she was fired from her job at the Montgomery Fair, she was told she was being laid off because the Christmas rush was over. Her husband, too, lost his job as a barber at the Maxwell Air Force Base. Not only was the Parks family experiencing the awful economic pinch of unemployment, but they were besieged by hate-filled phone calls. Night and day the phone rang. Callers threatened to kill Mrs. Parks. The family was wracked by tension, bringing about the complete physical breakdown of Mr. Parks.

For a while the MIA employed Mrs. Parks, sending her out to speak at schools and churches in order to raise money for the boycott. At other times she worked in the MIA office as a clerk, and she then became head of the welfare committee. She also took on odd jobs as a seamstress. To her brother's repeated pleas that the family join him in Detroit, where he lived and worked, she said no. Montgomery was her hometown, and that was where she wanted to be.

It became clear in those first few months of the movement

that the educated and articulate Reverend Martin Luther King, Jr., had emerged as the leader. Surrounding him was a group of skilled young aides, among them many ministers. These natural leaders continued their role in the community, acting like strong patriarchs, directing, advising, preaching.

The role of women in the boycott was not always appreciated. The male leadership simply assumed that women could not be leaders, though they were valued as assistants, secretaries, and clerks.

Women made up 56 percent of the total black population, and they were, in a way, the backbone of the movement. They not only trudged back and forth to work, but they ran their homes, shopped, and took care of the children, all without the advantage of bus transportation. They attended weekly meetings, always cheerful and committed to the struggle.

Women had also been the trailblazers of the movement. The protest was rooted in the bold "no" to segregated bus seating uttered by Mrs. Rosa Parks. Mrs. Jo Ann Robinson set the boycott into immediate motion. She was helped by her friends and colleagues in the Women's Political Council. Women were on the MIA executive board and active on the finance committee and in the car pool. And four hard-working, dedicated women were the paid staffers of the MIA. Women like Mrs. Georgia Gilmore, the mother of six children and a domestic worker, enlivened the weekly meetings with reports about their success in raising money for the boycott. Mrs. Gilmore, who had once been arrested for refusing to get off the front of a bus and reboard in the rear, organized a group of neighbors into the Club from Nowhere. Mrs. Inez Ricks organized the Friendly Club. Both women baked and sold cakes and pies to workers and cafeterias to raise money.

Everyone could see that something precious and miraculous

was emerging out of the protest movement. Montgomery's black citizens, once without hope, had bonded together and could feel their power. Changes were slowly taking place on other fronts. Backed by the Supreme Court decision desegregating schools, a student named Autherine Lucy made the first attempt to integrate Alabama schools when she entered the campus of the University of Alabama in Tuscaloosa. On her first day she was confronted with the mob violence of over one thousand white students who marched to the house of the university's president to demand that the university stay white.

Extremists got a boost from Senator James Eastland, the main speaker at the prosegregation rally held at Montgomery's largest arena, the state coliseum. Under a show of waving Confederate flags, and red, white, and blue colors, the Mississippi senator urged resistance to desegregation.

As blacks nevertheless made progress, racist terror continued to increase. To break the dangerous tug of war, white businessmen stepped in. Calling themselves the "Men of Montgomery," they tried to restore peace to the city. They sent delegations to meet with representatives of the MIA, but the two groups could not resolve their differences. For instance, the MIA suggested that only five seats be reserved for white riders, but the Men of Montgomery insisted on ten.

In the continuing struggle, a handful of white people remained staunch supporters of the boycott movement. Others fell by the wayside, unable to cope with the criticism of the white community. Two white women made known their early support in letters to the *Advertiser*. Frances P. McLeod suggested that Montgomery follow the lead of southern cities such as Nashville and Richmond that had a first-come seating arrangement on their buses. Mrs I. B. Rutledge, in her letter, wrote that many agreed with her that Negroes had as much right to bus seats as white people. The Reverend Thomas Thrasher, who voiced such ideas, found his white congregation staying away from his church.

Clifford and Virginia Durr made a stir in Montgomery by their outspoken support of integration and their friendship with black people. These two whites, born and raised in the Deep South of what was called "aristocratic stock," had resettled in Alabama after years in Washington, D.C., where Mr. Durr had held important posts in Roosevelt's New Deal administration. Through their work in interracial organizations and their friendship with Mrs. Parks, E. D. Nixon, and others, they were accepted in the black community. The white community could not completely isolate them because the Durr family was too steeped in the white upper class. Though Lucy Judkins Durr did not endorse her son's racial beliefs, neither did she cut him off from the family.

Both Virginia and Clifford Durr well knew the price that had to be paid for outspoken liberal ideas. Like others who suffered business losses as a result of white pressure, Mr. Durr's legal practice barely survived on the low-paying cases he handled. But he was helped by his brother, a successful Montgomery businessman; and to cut expenses in his law office, Virginia Durr became her husband's secretary.

Another unique person was the slender, blond Reverend Robert S. Graetz. A former missionary, he became minister of the all-black Trinity Lutheran Church on Cleveland Avenue in Montgomery. Dedicated and hardworking, he was the only white member of the MIA executive board. From the first days of the boycott, he was active as a volunteer, chauffeuring forty to fifty people a day to and from their jobs. As a member of the transportation committee, he helped organize the hundreds of vehicles that became the backbone of the car pool. Targeted by the police, he was arrested one day for running a taxi service but released after half an hour. He, his wife, and their two small children lived in the parsonage next door to the church. Asked why he put his life in danger to support the boycott, he replied, "I know that I shall be criticized for my stand. I may even suffer violence. But I cannot minister to souls alone. My people have bodies."

For his support of the boycott, angry whites twice slashed the tires on his car and poured sugar into the gasoline tank. Both his church and his home would bear the violence of the white community.

A tragic victim of persecution was a young white librarian, Juliette Morgan, the daughter of an old southern family. A brilliant young woman, she was elected to the honor society of Phi Beta Kappa during her studies at the University of Alabama. In letters to newspaper editors, she made known her firm convictions that segregation was an evil. In one such letter to the *Advertiser* she wrote, "One feels history is being made in Montgomery these days. It is hard to imagine a soul so dead, a heart so hard, a vision so blinded and provincial as not to be awed with admiration at the quiet dignity, discipline, and dedication with which Negroes have conducted the boycott." She compared the movement to Mahatma Gandhi's struggle against British rule in India, in which he used nonviolent resistance. In another letter she wrote, "I think that segregation is an evil that has limited our horizons and dwarfed our souls."

For her daring and outspoken support of the boycott, she became the target of segregationist hate groups, among them the White Citizens Council. They hounded her and demanded that she be fired from her job as reference librarian at the Montgomery Public Library. To put pressure on the city, white people boycotted the branch library where she worked. She received threatening phone calls both at her home and in the library. Rocks were thrown through the windows and she was insulted on the streets.

She refused to stand by and do nothing, but unfortunately she was not surrounded by a network of support. Hers was a lonely battle in a sea of hate. Bereft of friends, frail, and sensitive to the abuse, she suffered untold anguish . No one came to her defense. She took a leave of absence from her job and became increasingly a recluse. She died in the summer of 1957— apparently a suicide, for she left a note saying, "I can't go on."

In her memory her mother placed volumes of her letters and writings in the state archives in Montgomery, Alabama. As teacher, writer, and educator, she expressed her idealism and hope that "equal rights and respect for all people" would prevail.

9

# "A GREAT MOMENT OF HISTORY"

White officials tried a new tactic: mass arrests. In the eleventh week of the boycott, they pulled out a seldom-used state law against illegal organized boycotts, and on February 21 they rounded up 115 MIA leaders and members. Eighty-nine of these were indicted, charged with committing a crime. Though attention centered on Rosa Parks and the Reverend King, the assemblage included twenty-four ministers, among them Ralph B. Abernathy. Also in the group were Mrs. Jo Ann Robinson and the elderly Mrs. West. They were all fingerprinted and photographed with large numbers hung around their necks. As soon as the procedures were over, lawyers freed the prisoners on bond.

The boycott had been like a train chugging along, gradually picking up steam. The mass arrests acted like rocket fuel, shooting the movement forward. During the first months only black newspapers informed the country about the boycott, but after the arrests, newspaper reporters and television and radio commentators descended on Montgomery. They saw the drama of

the boycott and the personal heroism of those involved. They
wanted to know about leaders such as E. D. Nixon and Rufus
Lewis, and they were drawn to the magnetic Dr. Martin Luther
King, Jr., whom they wrote up as the man of the hour.

What's going on? they asked. They ferreted out background
material and sent the news around the world—to Rome, Lon-
don, Tokyo, South Africa, Australia. In India people eagerly read
about Dr. King, who, like their leader Gandhi, was taking up the
cause of nonviolent resistance. Television and radio began to
transmit regular up-to-date news of the boycott. Thousands of
pieces of mail were delivered to the MIA office as letters and
money poured in. Montgomery had won worldwide attention.

Black organizations throughout the country—professional
groups, sororities and fraternities, church groups—sent thousands of dollars. Trade unions announced their support. The
International Longshoremen's and Warehousemen's Union in
San Francisco sent in a $1,500 contribution, and one of its locals
pledged a $99.99 weekly contribution for ten weeks. They were
acting, they said, "in the true spirit of brotherhood, and know-
ing that an injury to one is an injury to all." A woman in Swit-
zerland sent in a $500 contribution with a letter, saying, "I feel
deeply ashamed for the white people to which I belong [sic]."
Tourists visited Montgomery to see for themselves what was
going on, considering the boycott a historic event. Five inmates
in a prison in Pennsylvania sent a dollar each to the MIA. And
the literary community made its support felt in contributions,
articles, interviews, and books.

The world learned about Rosa Parks, Martin Luther King, Jr.,
and the spirit of some fifty thousand people who, in the fourth
month of a bus boycott, remained strong and united. The mass
arrests pulled them still closer together and inspired them
anew. Five thousand showed up for the meeting the night of
the arrests. As usual, they began to arrive long before the hour.

They talked to each other and sang their favorite hymns, "On-ward, Christian Soldiers" and "Leaning on Everlasting Arms." Elegiac voices filled the church, filtering through the stained-glass windows to merge with the singing of the crowds out-doors.

After the prayer and scripture reading, Dr. King sounded a note of encouragement, reminding people how important it was to love rather than to hate. He talked in the special cadence he was developing, his voice deep, lyrical, repeating key phrases: "We have known humiliation, we have known abusive language.... And we decided to rise up only with the weapon of protest.... If we are arrested every day, if we are exploited every day, if we are trampled every day, don't let anyone pull you so low as to hate them.... This is not a war between the white and the Negro but a conflict between justice and injus-tice. We are not trying to improve the Negro of Montgomery, but the whole of Montgomery."

Changes had taken place within the city, and no one knew that better than Rosa Parks. In March 1956, she returned to the Highlander Folk School to give a talk at the second annual lecture series. The bus boycott was four months old, and Mrs. Parks opened her talk by saying that "Montgomery today is nothing at all like it was as you knew it last year." She stressed the unique unity among the black people. That unity was hold-ing firm, she said, in the face of months of difficulties and ha-rassment. It ruffled white officials to see that black people could be disciplined and could struggle to improve their conditions. Furthermore, she pointed out, Montgomery had become the center of worldwide attention. From all corners of the globe, money was coming in to support the boycott.

As the boycott became front-page news, northern organiza-tions sent delegates down to try to make the struggle national in scope and broaden its goals. Dr. King, too, had a sense of the widening impact of the movement. "We are caught in a great moment of history," he said at a mass meeting. "It is bigger than Montgomery. . . . The vast majority of the people of the world are colored. . . . We are part of that great movement" to be free, he said.

On Monday, March 19, the Reverend King was the first of those who had been indicted in the mass arrests to be brought to trial. Three days later, on March 22, he was found guilty as charged and fined $500 and $500 in court costs. He was freed on $1,000 bond; his lawyers planned to appeal the case. The others who were indicted would not be brought to trial until the appeal decision was handed down, a procedure that usually took a year.

The young minister, now twenty-seven, appeared to onlookers to be an older man. At first unprepared for the role into which he had been thrust, he had gone through periods of self-doubt. He had questioned his abilities and his courage. As the struggle wore on he became a strong and self-confident national leader, carrying his message of equality and justice to the church groups and political and social clubs before whom he spoke. He sounded the catchwords for the spirit of the boycott: unity, discipline, and nonviolent resistance.

The MIA itself had developed into an extremely efficient organization. By mid-April it had bought over fifteen station wagons for the car pool, making transportation more stable. Each one was registered in the name of a black church. The work of volunteers was slowly replaced by a paid staff of twenty full-time drivers and seventy-four part-time ones. Dispatchers were also put on salary, making procedures more reliable. The MIA tried to get a license from the city to operate a jitney, or small bus service. But the city rejected the application.

In April the movement was cheered by an unexpected piece of good news: The U.S. Supreme Court upheld a lower court ruling that segregated bus seating on city buses in Columbia, South Carolina, was unconstitutional. Though the South Carolina decision raised the morale of the boycotters, it split white officialdom in two. The Montgomery City Lines, owners of the buses, made a dramatic concession: Their drivers would no longer enforce segregated seating on city buses. But Mayor Gayle, on behalf of the city, declared that the segregation laws must be upheld.

The MIA began to understand the need for political power through the use of the ballot and it undertook a voter-registration campaign. "The chief weapon in our fight for civil rights is the vote," said Dr. King.

Finally, the Montgomery bus boycott movement won a stunning victory. In June the federal district court, before which the MIA had challenged segregated bus seating, declared segregated seating in Montgomery unconstitutional. While the black population celebrated the triumph, the city commissioners vowed to take the case to the United States Supreme Court, a slow, complex procedure.

In October, with the boycott in its tenth month, the city again tried to break the car-pool system. With no advance notice, officials cancelled the insurance policies on the station wagons. Without insurance, the cars could not operate. Again the black leadership outwitted city officials. Through the assistance of a black insurance agent in Atlanta, Georgia, arrangements were made for new policies.

In response to that victory, the segregationists moved on to another tactic. They got a court order from the state preventing blacks from gathering on street corners while waiting for a pickup, claiming that the congregation of people was a public nuisance.

Violence continued, this time directed at the home of the Reverend Graetz. Fortunately, neither he, his pregnant wife, nor their two small children were at home when the bomb struck, destroying part of the house. But the strain of nasty phone calls and threatening notes was taking its toll on the young family. They moved around so much to avoid danger that they no longer had a home.

When all else failed, the city took legal action against the car-pool system itself, asking the court to declare it illegal.

City lawyers were in the midst of arguing this case in court when word reached Dr. King that the United States Supreme Court had reached a decision in the case of the Montgomery bus boycott: It had declared Alabama state and city laws requiring segregation on buses unconstitutional.

Rosa Parks sits in the front of a Montgomery bus integrated by a federal court order (*Courtesy the* Montgomery Advertiser)

Rosa Parks with the Eleanor Roosevelt Woman of Courage Award (*Courtesy the Montgomery Advertiser*)

Virginia Durr, Fred Gray, and Rosa Parks singing "We Shall Overcome" at the twenty-fifth anniversary celebration of the bus boycott (*Courtesy the Montgom-ery Advertiser*)

Coretta Scott King kissing Rosa Parks after giving her the Martin Luther King, Jr., Nonviolent Peace Prize (*Courtesy the Montgomery Advertiser*)

The Civil Rights Monument in Montgomery, Alabama (*Courtesy the Alabama Bureau of Tourism and Travel*)

# 10

## "WHEN I WAS A CHILD . . ."

People wept at the news. They stood in the streets—women, men, and children—and wept. "We felt that we were somebody," was the way Jo Ann Robinson put it, "that we had forced the white man to give what we knew [was] our own citizenship." They wept not only at the victory but at the pain they had suffered: the bombings, the arrests, the harassment.

Rosa Parks would say years later, "I don't recall that I felt anything great about it. It didn't feel like a victory, actually. There still had to be a great deal to do."

The Reverend Graetz read the scriptures that evening at two mass meetings held in churches at either end of town. Quoting from the Bible, he said, "When I was a child, I spoke as a child, I understood as a child, I thought as a child; but when I became a man I put away childish things." The words brought a loud outburst of cheers from the congregation. People recognized how much they had changed, how much they had grown in the struggle.

But the struggle was not yet over, for the leadership had decided to call off the official protest immediately but to delay the return to the buses until the written order on desegregation arrived in the city of Montgomery. On the same day the desegregation ruling was handed down, Circuit Court Judge Eugene Carter announced his ruling putting an end to the car-pool system. He did so on the grounds that it was a "public nuisance" and a "private enterprise." With the car-pool system declared illegal, people took to the streets by the thousands.

Nor did city officials accept the desegregation order quietly. They immediately issued a statement saying, "[We] will not yield one inch, but will do all in our power to oppose the integration of the Negro race with the white race in Montgomery, and will forever stand like a rock against social equality, intermarriage, and mixing of the races under God's creation and plan."

That night forty carloads of hooded KKK members rode through the black community. Their plans to demonstrate were announced over the radio, and threats of bombings and violence were rampant. Dr. King's mail was unusually threatening, announcing that the KKK would "burn down fifty houses in one night, including yours."

The spirit of victory was not dimmed. Black people knew they had won the battle in the Supreme Court decision. When the Klan rode through the back streets of their neighborhoods, blacks defied them, standing quietly on their porches and on the streets as the Klan went by. Klan power had weakened that day, like dead leaves scattering in the wind.

To prepare for desegregation, the MIA launched several programs in churches and schools. In wide-ranging discussions, the point was made that desegregation was not a victory of blacks over whites but a victory for justice and democracy. It was a victory for all Montgomery, as Dr. King had hoped.

Fliers were distributed throughout the neighborhoods suggesting ways to integrate the buses. Among the suggestions was this one: "Do not deliberately sit by a white person, unless there is no other seat." And: "If cursed, do not curse back. If pushed, do not push back. If struck, do not strike back but evidence love and goodwill at all times."

No one prepared the white community for bus integration. On the contrary, a leader of the White Citizens Council threatened that any "attempt to enforce this decision will lead to riot and bloodshed."

On December 20, 1956, the written order for desegregation of buses reached Montgomery. One year and fifteen days had passed since the boycott had started. For a total of 381 days, 50,000 black people had waged a great rebellion. They won a battle not only over a social system but over their own fear of facing white power.

To pave the way for integrated seating, the ministers agreed that they would ride the buses for a few days. At 5:45 A.M. on the morning of December 21, Martin Luther King, Jr., Ralph Abernathy, E. D. Nixon, and a white friend, Glen Smiley, a representative of the Fellowship for Reconciliation, boarded a bus. Television crews and newspaper reporters recorded the event for history. It took place peacefully, as if nothing special were happening.

Rosa Parks, at the urging of a group of reporters, also integrated the bus that day. She took a seat in the front of the bus. What was she thinking? That it had taken a painful thirteen months of struggle and protest to make this simple event possible? That she could at last take any seat in a bus where she rightfully belonged as a citizen and as a human being?

The calm lasted a few days before random violence broke out. Snipers fired at buses; a fifteen-year-old teenager was beaten by five white men as she waited at a bus stop; a twenty-two-year-old pregnant black woman riding a bus, Mrs. Rosa

Jordan, was shot in both legs. A new round of bombings shattered neighborhoods, beginning with an attack on the home and church of Ralph Abernathy. Within a few hours bombs had destroyed the front of the Graetz home and also hit his church. This was the second bombing for Graetz in six months. In the series of attacks two more Baptist churches were destroyed. Though no one was hurt in the attacks, the damage was extensive and the effect was frightening.

For the first time groups of white people spoke out against the bombings. The Montgomery Advertiser asked the question, "Is it safe to live in Montgomery?" Several white ministers condemned the bombings as "un-Christian and uncivilized."

The city of Montgomery ordered the buses off the streets and established a midnight curfew for teenagers until the bombings stopped. In taking this step, the city was also punishing the bus company for accepting the order to desegregate seating. Despite this drastic order, the bombings continued. This time bombers struck at a black-owned taxi stand and at the home of a boycotter, a black hospital worker. Another attempt was made to bomb the Kings' home. Fortunately the family was away at the time, and the sticks of dynamite were discovered before they could explode.

Montgomery was in turmoil. To quiet both black and white residents, the city finally launched an investigation into the bombings, offering rewards for the arrest of the perpetrators. Seven men were arrested and two were brought to trial. Though evidence presented at the trial in January 1958 linked the men to the violence, the jury returned a verdict of not guilty.

The arrests resulted in the end of the bombings, and desegregated buses now rolled along the streets.

# "... UNTIL JUSTICE ROLLS DOWN LIKE WATERS ..."

L ooking back at the experience of her arrest years later, Rosa Parks would describe it to a group of college students as a trauma that she suffered both mentally and physically. She had always avoided becoming a public figure, but that evening's courageous act had thrust her into the spotlight. The shy woman had to speak before large audiences, meet with reporters and interviewers, and travel as a fund-raiser for the boycott movement.

Martin Luther King, Jr., called the boycott a "social revolution." No one in the movement remained the same. Dr. King would become the head of the Southern Christian Leadership Conference, a new organization headquartered in Atlanta, Georgia. Remaining in the forefront of the struggle, he would become the leader of the militant civil rights movement until his death from an assassin's bullet in 1968. He would take his place as a leading figure in United States history.

Both black and white residents of Montgomery were affected by the upheaval. A shift in social and economic values took place. Black people learned that from their unity came strength, and that they had purchasing power vital to the economy of the city. White merchants, banks, and businesses learned to respect that economic power and to treat it carefully. No longer were black customers shunted aside, treated rudely, and ignored. They were addressed by name and waited on, and their purchases were encouraged. It would take militant struggles before blacks could share in other public facilities such as water fountains, bathrooms, and lunch counters, but a beginning had been made.

And if the boycott was so successful in Montgomery, why not do the same in Birmingham and in Mobile? Other cities in the South used the boycott and other methods of nonviolent resistance to win changes in their regions.

Rosa Parks remained the great hero of the movement. The MIA honored her when it held its first annual Institute on Nonviolence and Social Changes in December 1957. The Reverend Abernathy, chair of the occasion, called the institute "Gandhi in America." Black and white social scientists and religious leaders read their papers before an audience of 1,500. Emerging from the conference was the fact that blacks had become leaders and that continued unity was essential to win new victories in the fight against segregation.

For Rosa Parks the Montgomery bus boycott brought a great upheaval in her way of life. In 1957 she, her husband, and her mother moved to Detroit, Michigan, to be near her brother. She had agreed to resettle when she found it difficult to find a job after being fired from the Montgomery Fair. It was a sad leave-taking, and one that E. D. Nixon regarded as most unfortunate. It seemed to him that she was a victim of the courageous act that had changed the city. She had stood up for the black community, he told an interviewer, but the community did not stand up for her. When the whites did not give her a job, the

MIA should have found steady employment for her. But Mrs. Parks did not share Mr. Nixon's feelings. As long as she was well, she commented, it was her "responsibility to do whatever I could for myself." At a farewell party, the community raised $800 to help her resettle.

The first few years in Detroit were also difficult for Mrs. Parks. Jobs were scarce for both her and her husband. For one year she left Detroit to work at the Hampton Institute in Virginia, sending home what she could from her salary. Not wanting to be separated from her family any longer, she returned to Detroit in 1958. That year her husband was hospitalized with pneumonia. The following year she was hospitalized with stomach ulcers.

Mrs. Parks had finally found work in a small tailoring shop when in 1965 she came to the attention of Congressman John Conyers, Jr., a newly elected Democratic member of the House of Representatives. He offered her employment in his Detroit office, where she worked first as a receptionist and then as a special aide.

Throughout her years in Detroit, Mrs. Parks has continued her activism: in the church as a deaconess of St. Matthew African Methodist Episcopal Church, in the NAACP, and also in the Southern Christian Leadership Conference, the organization first headed by Dr. Martin Luther King, Jr. And once again she committed herself to helping young people, counseling them about their rights and urging them to take advantage of every opportunity, no matter how small. Her own experience had taught her the importance of pushing on, of not falling by the wayside.

In the years when Mrs. Parks was finding it difficult to find a decent job, the public was acclaiming her a national hero. The story of the shy black woman who stood up to the rigid racist laws of the South, thereby starting a bus boycott and a crusade for justice, was being turned into legend. Reflecting the broad range of public appreciation for her unbroken record of civil rights activism, a long list of tributes and awards were bestowed on her. Here are a few of them.

In 1979 Mrs. Parks received the Spingarn Medal, the most prestigious award given by the National Association for the Advancement of Colored People. In making the award, Judge Damon J. Keith of the U.S. Sixth Circuit Court of Appeals, said, "Your courageous act on that quiet and cloudy day in Montgomery has secured your claim to immortality."

In 1980, at the twenty-fifth anniversary celebration of the bus boycott, a sixty-five-year-old Rosa Parks received the Martin Luther King, Jr., Nonviolent Peace Prize, the first woman recipient of the award. "It is so extraordinarily painful to look back on some of the things we went through," she said on that occasion. Mrs. Coretta Scott King, Dr. King's widow, in honoring Mrs. Parks called her "a woman whose courage and commitment have shaken the conscience of America."

A special tribute to Rosa Parks was held in New York City at a Broadway theater in June 1982, and in 1984 she was given the Eleanor Roosevelt Woman of Courage Award at a ceremony in New York's Plaza Hotel.

In 1985 she returned to Montgomery to celebrate the thirtieth anniversary of her arrest. She made it clear in her talk, as she has throughout her life, that she did not see herself as heroic but simply as a woman who took a stand against segregation. She could see the changes that had taken place in Montgomery over the years. It was no longer outwardly segregated. Signs separating the races had been removed. Hotels, bus stations, and public drinking fountains were integrated. Schools had both whites and blacks in attendance. Nevertheless the struggle to win full equality continues.

And the awards go on. In 1987 Mrs. Parks was given the Roger

E. Joseph Prize of the Jewish Institute of Religion for being the "mother of the modern Freedom Movement." More than two thousand people attended the services at Temple Emanu-El in New York City, at which she was given a cash award of $10,000. It would go toward the founding of the Rosa and Raymond Parks Institute for Self-Development, which Mrs. Parks was planning in Detroit. The institute would offer guidance to black youths in preparation for leadership and careers.

In 1987, after more than twenty years, Mrs. Parks retired from her job in Representative Conyers's office. The congressman was at her side in February 1990 when her seventy-seventh birthday was celebrated in Washington, D.C. She was hailed as a pioneer of the Civil Rights Movement. The 3,000 people in the Kennedy Center and the several hundred at a pregala dinner raised funds for her institute in Detroit.

The Rosa Parks story has also found its way into dance, theater, music, film, and literature. A Philadelphia dance group, Philadanco, performed in New York City in April 1990. On the program was a dance called "Rosa" that dealt with the "courage of those who dare to be different." The dance communicated the loneliness of the fight against the established order.

Now on view at the National Portrait Gallery in Washington, D.C., is a bronze sculpture of Mrs. Parks unveiled at the end of February 1991. The bust, by Artis Lane, places Mrs. Parks among the country's most famous and accomplished citizens.

The country needs to see and hear Mrs. Parks. She stands out as a symbol of courage and of the continuing fight to make democracy work in the United States. While Mrs. Parks tries to fulfill some of the many demands made on her, she links her name with struggles worldwide, such as the fight against apartheid in South Africa.

Three flags now fly over the state capitol in Montgomery, Alabama. On the top of the flagpole flies the Stars and Stripes.

Below it is the Confederate flag, and below that the state flag.

The Confederate flag is a continuous reminder of the laws and customs of the old South, a reminder that Montgomery was the Cradle of the Confederacy. But Montgomery has also become known as the cradle of the modern Civil Rights Movement. Built to commemorate that movement and its heroes and martyrs is a simple but powerful sculpture. It stands in a plaza in front of the Southern Poverty Law Center, a nonprofit, public-interest organization located just below the state capitol and close to the Dexter Avenue Baptist Church.

Every week hundreds of schoolchildren and other visitors come to see the memorial. Etched on a large, black disk are key events of the Civil Rights Movement and the names of forty men and women who died in the struggle. Rosa Parks is listed as a leader of the Montgomery bus boycott. Over the disk perpetually flows a thin sheet of water. In back of the disk is a nine-foot-high curved black granite wall. Engraved onto the wall, beneath a sheet of water also perpetually flowing, are Dr. King's words chosen from the Bible and first spoken at the mass meeting at the Holt Street Baptist Church on December 5, 1955. "We will not be satisfied," he said,

> ". . . until justice rolls down like waters and righteousness like a mighty stream."

# ACKNOWLEDGMENTS

I am grateful to Virginia Foster Durr for facilitating my research during my visit to Montgomery, Alabama. I would also like to thank several of the women in Montgomery who shared their experiences with me, among them Mrs. Jewette Anderson, Mrs. Bertha Butler, Mrs. Johnnie Carr, Mrs. Mattie Lee Langford, and Mrs. Mary Jo Smiley.

My special thanks to Keeta Kendall, state librarian of Montgomery's Department of Archives and History, for making archival material accessible.

As always, I am dependent on the cooperation of librarians for my research, and I would like to thank the staff of the Schomburg Center for Research in Black Culture in New York City.

# BIBLIOGRAPHY

An extensive literature exists on the subject of the Montgomery bus boycott, ranging from scholarly texts to popular articles. These are a few selected sources from my research:

Juan Williams, *Eyes on the Prize* (New York: Viking, 1987) and the film by the same title are invaluable overviews of the civil rights years.

Dealing with the role of Martin Luther King, Jr., are two essential books: *Bearing the Cross*, by David J. Garrow (New York: William Morrow and Co., 1986), and Taylor Branch's *Parting the Waters* (New York: Simon and Schuster, 1988).

Personal memoirs and autobiographies give special insights, and I here mention three distinguished books: the memoir of Jo Ann Gibson Robinson, *The Montgomery Bus Boycott and the Women Who Started It* (Knoxville: University of Tennessee Press, 1987); Martin Luther King, Jr.'s *Stride Toward Freedom* (New York: Harper and Row, 1958); and Virginia Foster Durr's *Outside the Magic Circle* (Tuscaloosa: University of Alabama Press, 1985).

Important material was found in Lamont H. Yeakey's unpublished Ph.D. dissertation, "The Montgomery, Alabama, Bus Boycott, 1955–56" (Columbia University, 1979).

Invaluable to my research were the many interviews granted by Mrs. Parks that have appeared in newspapers, periodicals, and books. Here are a few of them: Lerone Bennett, Jr., writes about "The Day the Black Revolution Began" in *Ebony* magazine (vol. 32, September 1977). Vernon Jarrett, in a series in the *Chicago Tribune* (November 30 to December 4, 1975) deals with "The Forgotten Heroes of the Montgomery Bus Boycott." Howell Raines has an interview with Mrs. Parks in *My Soul Is Rested* (New York: G. P. Putnam's Sons, 1977). Arthur E. Thomas in *Like It Is*, edited by Emily Rovetch (New York: E. P. Dutton, 1981), interviewed leaders in black America. Also interesting were the comments made by Mrs. Parks to Earl and Miriam Selby for their book, *Odyssey, Journey Through Black America* (New York: G. P. Putnam's Sons, 1971).

Adding a personal dimension to my research were the visuals that can be viewed at the Schomburg Center for Research in Black Culture. In addition to the film "Eyes on the Prize," there are, among others, Gil Noble's "An Amazing Grace" and a film called "Martin Luther King, Jr.: From Montgomery to Memphis," put out by Bailey Film Associates.

# SUGGESTED TITLES FOR YOUNG READERS

Cook, Fred J. *The Ku Klux Klan, America's Recurring Nightmare*. New York: Julian Messner, 1980.

Harris, Janet. *The Long Freedom Road: The Civil Rights Story*. New York: McGraw-Hill Book Co., 1967.

Jakoubek, Robert. *Martin Luther King, Jr.* New York: Chelsea House, 1989.

Schulke, Flip, editor. *Martin Luther King, Jr.: A Documentary . . . Montgomery to Memphis*. New York: W. W. Norton & Co., 1976.

Severn, Bill. *The Right to Vote*. New York: Ives, Washburn, Inc., 1972.

Sterling, Dorothy. *Tear Down the Walls: A History of the American Civil Rights Movement*. New York: Doubleday and Company, 1968.

Stevenson, Janet. *The Montgomery Bus Boycott, December, 1955*. New York: Franklin Watts, Inc., 1971.

# INDEX

Page numbers in *italics* refer to illustrations.

Teachers in civil rights movement, 29–30, 37, 39, 71–72
Tennessee, 29
Thrasher, Rev. Thomas, 70
Till, Emmett, 30
Transportation alternatives, 39–40, 43, 58–59, 76, 77, 85
Trinity Lutheran Church, 70
Tuscaloosa, Alabama, 69

**U**
Unions, labor, 35–36, 74
University of Alabama, 69, 71
U.S. Supreme Court rulings, 28, 69, 76–77, 78, 85

**V**
Violence
    against African-Americans, 17, 19, 20, 30, 33, 45, 64–65, 86–87
    against white activists, 71–72, 77–78
Voter registration, 18, 19, 20, 77

**W**
Washington, D.C., 70, 92
West, Mrs. A. W., 57, 59
    arrest of, 73
White, Miss Alice L., 18
White Citizens Council, 28–29, 33, 62, 71, 86
Whites as activists, 29, 36, 37, 45, 69, 70, 71–72, 77–78
Williams, Mrs. Mary Lucy, 64
Women's Political Council, 37–38, 68
Women's role in civil rights, 68
World War II, 28, 39